WITCHES VS. GENIES

Disclaimer:

The creatures in this book are not real. They are from myths. They are fun to imagine. Read the 45th Parallel Press series Magic, Myth, and Mystery to learn more about them.

45TH PARALLEL PRESS

Published in the United States of America by Cherry Lake Publishing
Ann Arbor, Michigan
www.cherrylakepublishing.com

Reading Adviser: Marla Conn, MS, Ed., Literacy specialist, Read-Ability Inc.
Book Designer: Melinda Millward

Photo Credits: © Pushkin/Shutterstock.com, back cover, 10; © Evgeniia Litovchenko/Shutterstock.com, cover, 5; © Gluiki/Shutterstock.com, cover, 5; © Kiselev Andrey Valerevich/Shutterstock.com, cover, 5, 29; © Marcin Sylwia Ciesielski/Shutterstock.com, 6; © Irina Alexandrovna/Shutterstock.com, 9; © Radnatt/canstockphoto.com, 12; © Iuliia Stepashova/Shutterstock.com, 15; © Ricardo Romero/Shutterstock.com, 16; © camilkuo/Shutterstock.com, 19; © GraphicsRF/Shutterstock.com, 19, 20; © vectortatu/Shutterstock.com, 20; © Kolbakova Olga/Shutterstock.com, 21; © fergregory/istockphoto.com, 23; © pic0bird/Shutterstock.com, 24; © Timothy L Barnes/Shutterstock.com, 25; © tatui suwat/Shutterstock.com, 25; © Wonman Kim/Getty Images, 27

Graphic Element Credits: © studiostoks/Shutterstock.com, back cover, multiple interior pages; © infostocker/Shutterstock.com, back cover, multiple interior pages; © mxbfilms/Shutterstock.com, front cover; © MF production/Shutterstock.com, front cover, multiple interior pages; © AldanNi/Shutterstock.com, front cover, multiple interior pages; © Andrii Symonenko/Shutterstock.com, front cover, multiple interior pages; © acidmit/Shutterstock.com, front cover, multiple interior pages; © manop/Shutterstock.com, multiple interior pages; © Lina Kalina/Shutterstock.com, multiple interior pages; © mejorana/Shutterstock.com, multiple interior pages; © NoraVector/Shutterstock.com, multiple interior pages; © Smirnov Viacheslav/Shutterstock.com, multiple interior pages; © Piotr Urakau/Shutterstock.com, multiple interior pages; © IMOGI graphics/Shutterstock.com, multiple interior pages; © jirawat phueksriphan/Shutterstock.com, multiple interior pages

45th Parallel Press is an imprint of Cherry Lake Publishing.

Library of Congress Cataloging-in-Publication Data

Names: Loh-Hagan, Virginia, author.
Title: Witches vs. genies / by Virginia Loh-Hagan.
Other titles: Witches versus genies
Description: Ann Arbor, Michigan : Cherry Lake Publishing, 2020. | Series: Battle royale : lethal warriors | Includes index.
Identifiers: LCCN 2019032883 (print) | LCCN 2019032884 (ebook) | ISBN 9781534159358 (hardcover) | ISBN 9781534161658 (paperback) | ISBN 9781534160507 (pdf) | ISBN 9781534162808 (ebook)
Subjects: LCSH: Witches—Juvenile literature. | Jinn—Juvenile literature.
Classification: LCC BF1566 .L643 2020 (print) | LCC BF1566 (ebook) | DDC 133.4/3—dc23
LC record available at https://lccn.loc.gov/2019032883
LC ebook record available at https://lccn.loc.gov/2019032884

Printed in the United States of America
Corporate Graphics

About the Author

Dr. Virginia Loh-Hagan is an author, university professor, and former classroom teacher. She wrote a 45th Parallel Press book about the Salem witch trials. She lives in San Diego with her very tall husband and very naughty dogs. To learn more about her, visit www.virginialoh.com.

Table of Contents

Introduction

Imagine a battle between witches and genies. Who would win? Who would lose?

Enter the world of *Battle Royale: Lethal* **Warriors**! Warriors are fighters. This is a fight to the death! The last team standing is the **victor**! Victors are winners. They get to live.

Opponents are fighters who compete against each other. They challenge each other. They fight with everything they've got. They use weapons. They use their special skills. They use their powers.

They're not fighting for prizes. They're not fighting for honor. They're fighting for their lives. Victory is their only option.

Let the games begin!

VS.

WITCHES

Some witches have moles. They have birthmarks. They have scars. These are called devil's marks.

Witches are special humans. They practice magic. They have powers. They have skills. There are many kinds of witches. Some practice **light magic**. This is good magic. They help people. Some practice **dark magic**. They harm people. Witch doctors heal. They use things from nature. They fight against evil spirits. Sea witches command the sea. They control the moon. They control tides. They control weather. They steer ships. They decide seamen's fate. Traditional witches work with **spirits**. Spirits are from another world.

Some witches are pretty. Some are ugly. Some change. Some look like people. Some look like monsters. Witches come in all shapes. They come in all sizes.

Covens are groups of witches. Most covens have 13 witches. Witches meet. They get together. They do witchcraft. Some witches work alone. They're called hedge witches.

Witches **cast spells**. They create magical actions. There are different spells. Spells banish. They repel. They protect. They harm. Witches **hex**. Hex means to give curses. They wish for bad things. They also give **blessings**. Blessings are good wishes. Witches make **potions**. Potions are special mixes. They poison people. They make people do things. Love potions are popular. Witches use **charms**. These are magical objects. They have power. They do specific tasks.

Sorcerers are the most powerful magicians. Wizards are second. Witches are third.

Some witches have **psychic** powers. Psychic means the mind. These witches see the past. They see the future. They read minds. They **scry**. Scrying is gazing. Witches gaze into crystal balls. They gaze into mirrors. They gaze into candles. They gaze into water. They wait for **visions**. Visions are signs. They're messages.

Some witches have animals. These animals are **familiars**. They're more than pets. They serve their witches. They do things witches can't. They go places witches can't.

Witches have a **creed**. A creed is a rule. It's the "threefold law." Witches can do evil deeds. But the evil comes back. It comes back 3 times more. This means for every 1 evil thing they do, 3 bad things will happen to them.

FUN FACTS ABOUT WITCHES

- Moll Dyer died around 1697. She lived in Leonardtown, Maryland. She was accused of being a witch. People set her house on fire. Dyer ran away. It was a cold winter. Her frozen body was found on a rock. Dyer's ghost haunts the land. She looks for the men who killed her. On really cold nights, people see Dyer's ghost.
- Sometimes healers wrote "cat's paw" or "snake's tongue" as ingredients. People thought they were spells or potions. But these words were really codes. Healers disguised the names of herbs and other plants. They didn't want others to know their recipes. But this made people think they were witches.
- Witches were around in ancient times. Hecate was a Greek goddess. She was the goddess of witchcraft. She created the jinx. Jinx is bad luck.
- People hunted witches. They burned them. They stoned them. They drowned them. Over 60,000 people were killed. They were accused of being witches. This happened between 1480 and 1750. This happened in Europe and North America.

GENIES

Genies can live anywhere as long as they're in their vessels.

Genies are magical beings. They live in **vessels**. Vessels are containers. Some live in bottles. Some live in **oil lamps**. Oil lamps hold oil. They make light. They use oil to do this. Genies are **imprisoned**. They're trapped inside. They can be trapped for years. They're trapped until someone finds the vessel. When the vessel is rubbed, the genie is released.

Genies **grant** 3 wishes to their **masters**. Grant means to give. Masters are people who find the genies. They're in charge of the genies. Then, genies return to their vessels. They wait until they're found again.

Genies come in all shapes and sizes. They have thick fur on their legs. Some have **hooves**. Hooves are hard coverings over feet. Some genies have heads without bodies. Some have bodies without heads. Some are half-human. They have human bodies. They have fog for legs. Some genies have **tattoos**. These are colored ink designs on skin.

Genies can do many things. They make objects appear and disappear. They can change their shapes. They can become people. They can become animals. They can become fire. They can become air. They can become water.

Genies change when they use their powers. Their tattoos move on their skin.

Some genies can make themselves invisible. Some genies can read people's minds. Some genies trick people. Some genies take over people's bodies. They mess with people's lives. They change people's moods. Some genies can fly. Some genies change people's wishes. They twist people's words.

Genies have weaknesses. They can't travel far from their vessels. They can't talk to the dead. They can't bring people to life. They can't force people to fall in love. They can't kill. But they can give weapons or powers. They can attack. They can cause pain. Destroying a vessel is the only way to kill a genie. But vessels are hard to destroy.

FUN FACTS ABOUT GENIES

- Antoine Galland was a French man. He owned a copy of *The Arabian Nights*. He was the first person to translate the book. He did this in 1704. He changed "jinn" to "genie." The word "genie" comes from a Latin word. The Latin word is "genius." A genius is a guardian spirit of people and places.

- Ancient Romans believed in genies. Their genies watched over men. They caused men's actions. They appeared at birth. Evil genies fought good genies for control of a man's fate.

- Some people think genies have special colors. Blue genies are older and smart. Yellow genies are leaders. Green genies are young and playful. Black genies are powerful. Red genies are dangerous.

- Some stories say there are genies living in the Bermuda Triangle. Some genies live on the seafloor. These genies live in their bottles or lamps for a very long time.

CHOOSE YOUR BATTLEGROUND

Witches and genies are fierce fighters. They're well-matched. They both have similar powers. They both can do magic. Witches practice magic. Genies are magical beings. But they have different ways of fighting. They also have different weaknesses. So, choose your battleground carefully!

Battleground #1: Sea

- There are sea witches. They'd be comfortable fighting in the sea. But not all witches would. Some witches get seasick. But they can make themselves potions to feel better. Some witches hate water. Water melts them. Some witches can't cross water.

- Genies go where their vessels go. Some genies have lived at the bottom of the sea. They're part of buried treasure from shipwrecks.

Some genies like living in dirty places. They live in graveyards, garbage dumps, and bathrooms.

Battleground #2: Land

• Witches live on land. They live in homes. They live in cities. Many blend in with regular humans. Many witches know a lot about herbs. They can live off the land.

• Genies are used to living inside small spaces. They'd welcome being on land. They'd have lots of room to fight. They can float and move around.

Battleground #3: Mountains

• Witches and genies would be fine on mountains. Many genies and witches are used to living alone. They're used to living away from people. The thin air would not affect them. Both witches and genies can use magic to make themselves comfortable.

ARMED AND DANGEROUS: WEAPONS

Witches: Witches' greatest power is casting spells. Witches can create all kinds of magic. They say special words. The words become magic. Sometimes, witches add actions. These actions are called rituals. Sometimes, witches use objects. For example, they use dolls of people. They stick things on the doll. This causes harm to the person. Sometimes, witches use magical herbs and potions. Necromancy is the darkest of all magic. It's the practice of raising the dead.

Genies: Their greatest power is being invisible. Genies look like smoke. They're a mix of light and energy. They can't be seen. They vanish into the air. They can also hide in their lamps. They can control their invisibility. This means they can be invisible whenever they want. They can also control who sees them. They can be seen by some people and be invisible to others.

FIGHT ON!

The battle begins! It's Halloween night. This is a special night. The **veil** between the living and the dead is thin. A veil is like a gate. This means all **supernatural** beings can roam with the living. Supernatural means not of this world. Witches and genies are the most powerful at this time.

Move 1:

A master has collected multiple lamps. He rubs them. He wishes for the genies to **banish** witches from his town. Banish means to get rid of. The genies work together. The witches don't want to leave town. They're prepared to fight the genies.

Genies' vessels are often made of gold or silver.

Move 2:

Witches hide in plain sight. They look human. So, they blend in. They practice casting spells in secret. They don't want the genies to find them. They want time to do their spells. The coven breaks up into groups. One group practices spells to find the genies' vessels. They want to destroy the vessels. Another group practices spells to take away the genies' magic.

Move 3:

Genies fly around. They become invisible. They don't want to be seen. They look in houses. They look in dark corners. They sprinkle water on people who they think are witches. They're trying to get the witches to identify themselves. Witches don't like water. It burns their skin.

Some witches fly. They fly on brooms. They fly on animals.

LIFE SOURCE: FOOD FOR BATTLE

Witches: Witches drink "witches' brew." A brew is something that is made by mixing things together. Witches also use their brew for magic spells. A popular ingredient of a witches' brew is the eye of a newt. Newts are salamanders. They look like little lizards. They spend part of the year on land. They spend part of the year in water. They return to the water to have babies.

Genies: People aren't sure what genies eat. Some people think genies eat bones. When humans eat meat, they leave the bones. They let the bones dry out. Genies eat these bones. The dry bones become fresh again. They grow meat when eaten by genies. Some people think genies don't eat or drink at all.

Move 4:

Witches throw out witch dust. This reveals the shape of the genies. The witches say a spell out loud. They zap out energy. This energy is a beam of heat. It's like lightning.

Move 5:

Genies blink. They create a shield. The shields **deflect** the beams. Deflect means to bounce off. The beams hit the witches. Genies throw iron objects. Witches hate iron. Iron weakens their magic.

Move 6:

Witches stand in a circle. They hold hands. They're stronger when they do magic together.

People shouldn't wish for a genie's freedom. If they do, they'll take the place of the genie.

AND THE VICTOR IS . . .

What are their next moves?
Who do you think would win?

Witches could win if:

- They hide behind closed doors. Genies can't open doors. They also can't untie knots.
- They dip a silver knife into lamb's blood. Then, they put it inside the genies' vessels. Together, silver and lamb's blood weakens genies.

Genies could win if:

- They avoid the "witching hour." This time is between 3:00 a.m. and 4:00 a.m. Witches are the most powerful at this time.
- They make a "witch's bottle." This bottle will protect them. Genies need to fill a jar with sharp things. Then, they need to put some of their own hair in it. They need to bury it. Genies will be safe if the bottle stays buried and unbroken.

Both genies and witches can control weather.

Witches: Top Champion

Circe was from Greek myths. She was a witch. She was the goddess of magic. She was the daughter of a sun god and a sea nymph. She grew magical herbs. She made magical potions. She cast spells. She used a magical staff. She changed humans into wolves, lions, and pigs. She did this when she got mad. She did this to get revenge. For example, a king didn't want to date her. So, she turned him into a woodpecker. In another example, she fell in love with a sea god. The sea god chose Scylla instead. Scylla was a sea nymph. Circe got jealous. She poisoned the waters where Scylla bathed. She turned Scylla into a sea monster. Scylla had 12 feet. She had 6 long necks. She had 6 heads with sharp teeth. She kidnapped sailors from their ships. She ate them alive.

Genies: Top Champion

Shayatin were from Islamic stories. They were special genies. They represented evil. They represented ugliness. Some genies were good. But all shayatin were evil. They didn't do any good deeds. A group of shayatin were controlled by a leader. When their leader died, they all died. Shayatin were created from the smoke of fires. (Genies were created from a fire's blaze. Angels were created from a fire's light.) Shayatin were also formed from the blood of a murdered person. The only way to stop shayatin from forming was to hammer an unused silver nail into the blood. Shayatin controlled people by whispering to them. They tempted people to do bad things. People said special sayings to keep shayatin away. Shayatin lived in hell. They were both male and female. They couldn't marry. They took human shape. Their feet had hooves. They made people sick.

Consider This!

THINK ABOUT IT!

- How are witches and genies alike? How are they different? Are they more alike or different? Why do you think so?
- Would you rather fight a genie or witch? Explain your answer.
- What skills do you have to fight a genie? What skills do you have to fight a witch?
- What would you ask a genie or witch to do for you? What would be your wishes or requests?
- Read the 45th Parallel Press books about witches and genies. What more did you learn about these creatures?

LEARN MORE!

- Loh-Hagan, Virginia. *Genies*. Ann Arbor, MI: Cherry Lake Publishing, 2017.
- Loh-Hagan, Virginia. *Witches*. Ann Arbor, MI: Cherry Lake Publishing, 2016.
- Marsico, Katie. *Magic Monsters: From Witches to Goblins*. Minneapolis, MN: Lerner Publications, 2016.
- Napoli, Donna Jo, and Christina Balit (illustr.). *Tales from the Arabian Nights: Stories of Adventure, Magic, Love, and Betrayal*. Washington, DC: National Geographic, 2016.
- Steer, Dugald. *Wizardology: The Book of the Secrets of Merlin*. Cambridge, MA: Candlewick Press, 2005.

GLOSSARY

banish (BAN-ish) to kick out, to get rid of
blessings (BLES-ingz) good wishes
cast (KAST) to cause, to make something happen
charms (CHAHRMZ) magical objects
covens (KUH-venz) groups of vampires or witches
creed (KREED) rule
dark magic (DAHRK MAJ-ik) magic used to do evil deeds
deflect (dih-FLEKT) to bounce off
familiars (fuh-MIL-yurz) animals that serve witches
grant (GRANT) to give
hex (HEKS) to curse
hooves (HOOVZ) hard covering on animal feet
imprisoned (im-PRIZ-uhnd) jailed, trapped
light magic (LITE MAJ-ik) magic used to do good deeds
masters (MAS-turz) people who are in charge
oil lamps (OIL LAMPS) containers that hold oil used as fuel to make light
opponents (uh-POH-nuhnts) fighters who compete against each other
potions (POH-shuhnz) special mixes that create magic
psychic (SYE-kik) of the mind
scry (SKRYE) to gaze and tell the future
spells (SPELZ) series of words that have magical powers
spirits (SPIR-its) beings from another world
supernatural (soo-pur-NACH-ur-uhl) being beyond the laws of nature, magical
tattoos (tah-TOOZ) colored ink designs on skin
veil (VAYL) gate
vessels (VES-uhlz) containers that hold something
victor (VIK-tur) the winner
visions (VIZH-uhnz) signs or messages
warriors (WOR-ee-urz) fighters

INDEX